For

Helen Oppenheimer

with affection and

appreciation for

a special time shared.

8 September
Holy Family
Hartford, Connecticut

©1983 Forward Movement Publications,
412 Sycamore Street, Cincinnati, Ohio 45202.
Printed in U.S.A.

ISBN 0-88028-022-0

NOW IS THE ACCEPTED TIME

NOW IS THE ACCEPTED TIME

Writings & Prayers of

STEPHEN F. BAYNE, Jr.

FORWARD MOVEMENT PUBLICATIONS

CINCINNATI, OHIO

COMPILER'S NOTE

This is a book of how to live in the present time. It began with the idea of making accessible some of the writings and prayers of Bishop Stephen Bayne (1908-1974) who had a rare sense of time and history, who said his prayers and taught others to say theirs, who had a prophetic vision of God's Church and her mission. It developed naturally around the theme of *time* because to be with Stephen Bayne was to share the eternal in the moment.

The writings come from many periods of Stephen Bayne's life and show his use of the commonplace to invoke the divine. The prayers are his own — informed by many sources, notably Lancelot Andrewes, his chosen tutor. The cycles of prayer consecrate time somewhat as the monastic "hours" did — and thus bless the day. The "Dial of Parables" was distilled in the sleepless nights of the last months of Stephen Bayne's life, and has not been published before.

My thanksgiving for Stephen Bayne and his lifegiving ministry led to the sifting of these bits from the vast collection of his work. May they help us to redeem our time and to say our prayers.

Wilbur Charles Woodhams

September, 1982

Open our eyes, Lord Jesus,
to see you in our time;
Open our ears to hear you speak;
Open our hearts to love you
and all men because of you
and in you.

Now is the accepted time
II Corinthians 6:2

This is the first and most fundamental of the gifts of the spiritual life: the ability to "take time seriously," to consecrate time, to consecrate our little choices, to look at each day and each act in the light of eternity. That gift of God is what redeems us and our life. And in a world and in a time which feels itself to be so unredeemed and so unredeemable, what greater gift have we, in turn, to give the nations of the world except the gift of freedom and of consecrated choices by which we accept and live up to God's vocation of us?

Our choices are often particularly hard these days; and our minutes are filled with anxieties and distractions almost beyond number. God's gift to us is the ability to take our choices as they come, and to reflect on the great vocation that runs through them all, and then make them with a peaceful heart because we never lose sight of Him who is our goal. Look for Him every day, and make your choices with Him, so that His freedom, which He means to give you, may be yours.

✠ O God, Inspirer of the world's joy, Bearer of the world's pain, make us glad that we are men and women and that we have inherited the world's burdens. Deliver us from the luxury of cheap melancholy, and at the heart of our travail and uncertainty let unconquerable gladness dwell.

A starting place

Self-acceptance is certainly the first of our spiritual requirements. This is not in any mood of determinism, nor in any mood of fatalism at all. I am always troubled whenever we use the phrase "self-acceptance" lest we seem to give the impression that we Christians are fatalists, that the thing to do is simply accept the way you are and the conditions under which you are, and that is the end of it. This is very far from true; and I think the saving phrase always has to be put in there: "self-acceptance of yourself as you are, *as a starting place.*" Where you go is still the matter that you've got to choose. What you do about the conditions under which you live is up to you. Self-acceptance is where you begin, with you as you are, in the world you live in, facing the conditions that you do.

The second requirement is that we make of our day-by-day choices *our dialogue with God* — that we realize that because we are His creation, there is, therefore, nothing that can happen to us which is not known to Him and is not of concern to Him.

Then, third, the secret of *offering*, and of the service, the humble, penitent service, which leads us to bring our choices and lay them at the feet of the great High Priest, Who offers them.

✠ It's no use pretending we are somebody else. Use us, Lord, just as we are, when and how you see best.

How can we know the way?
St. John 14:5-15

I watched my wife threading a needle, a while ago. I think I have never outgrown a kind of childish wonder at this. I don't know whether other men feel as I do — I simply cannot do it. I watched her lick the end of the thread and then twirl it into a point, and into the eye of the needle it went without a whimper. And I thought of all the times I had tried to do that. Man can do a lot of things — bait a fish-hook or hurl a satellite around the world or write a sermon — but to thread a needle is one of the most astonishingly delicate and difficult things I know.

Sometimes we get the thread so wet that it goes all limp and leans over and bashfully refuses to go through the needle's eye at all. Or again we get a point, and pull the point through, and then find that only part of the thread is coming through and the rest of it curls up in a ball. In either case, we end up wishing that the thread would only want to go through the eye of the needle. It won't be forced through. It can't be pulled through. Only a desire to go through will do the trick. And cotton thread doesn't have any desires, apparently, and nobody knows — at least I don't — how to give it a desire.

Human beings do have desires. We are a bundle of them. But I think sometimes we act just like thread and a needle. We come up against a choice, a decision, a crisis in life, which is the eye of the needle God is trying to thread, and then we collapse, we simply refuse to make a positive decision, we just curl up limply, and no amount of persuasion will get us to come to a point and go through the choice ahead of us. Or else part of us will want to go through, and then the rest of us doesn't want to, and rolls up into a porcupine of confused desires and hopes, and the choice is only half made, with half of us assenting to it and the other half refusing. We love God with part of ourselves, but the rest of us will have nothing to do with Him.

One of the great Collects in the Prayer Book puts all this into a lovely phrase. "Grant unto thy people, that they may love the thing which thou commandest, and desire that which thou dost promise." This prayer gets to the heart of the business of making a person. To bring all our desires, all our wants and wishes, together under one supreme desire, so that we are one whole person and not a bundle of bits and pieces of half a dozen different people — this is the heart of it.

✠   Let our thoughts, Lord, be of you and lead to you.

Not to be offended
St. John 15:26-16:4

This passage reminds us of the purpose of much of Jesus' teaching, particularly in these last hours before the crucifixion. He lifts the curtain on the future — not at all because He wants to amaze or trouble His disciples, but rather in order to prepare them for the trial they themselves must meet. He cannot give them courage in advance. But He can lodge at least some of these things in their memory, so that when the time comes, and they are tested, they will have something firm and sure to hang on to.

This is part of their preparation for mission and ministry. One of the most perilous challenges to Christian discipleship anytime, anywhere, is the bewilderment that the world's scepticism and hostility creates. We suddenly, terribly, suspect that we have lost our way — that we are out of touch with reality — that there is no sense to our witness. Jesus meant that this should not happen. He meant that we should not be lost and terrified. All this is signified by the word "offended."

But the assurance is something deeper than merely His predictions of the future. The disciples will indeed remember that He told them of what they would have to meet. But they would also know that, in meeting it, they were sharing His own ministry. This is, no doubt, the greater glory of discipleship. It is something to know that He foresaw the coming tests. It is far more to know that He also bore them and bears them. He intends not only to reassure us but to unite us to Himself.

When you watch the struggle of the young Church, valiantly bearing its witness in the face of the hostile majority, you may indeed pray with confidence for those disciples. He is in the thick of this Himself.

✠   Help me to build this day on Thee, O Lord, Like a man building a house on rock, that I may be sure and steady in what I do for Thee and not shaken from my duty for fear of Thine enemies.

Easter souls
Philippians 1:19-21

It was a nifty day, wasn't it? Easter, we mean. There were crowds of attractively decorated people in evidence, and it was a magnificent day.

But we could not help reflecting on the distasteful fact that those very damsels and their escorts, and we ourselves for that matter, had the same stubborn, savage, sour mirror to face when we got ready to go to bed. New hats or no, we are the same old fruppy souls as on Easter Even. We are not, alas, magically changed by our apparel; the hands are the hands of Esau or Bonwit Teller right enough, but the voice is still Jacob's.

Nor have we the right, in this mortal life, to ask anything else. A new self — this "Christ who is our life" — does not come painlessly or magically. One self, one life, is quite enough for one soul; and it is our old self, tarnished and tired still, which by God's continual help is transformed as we bring His good desires to good effect. And we take deep courage from that reflection, really, once we get over the childish superstition that life is easy. It is not that; it is measured truly by the Cross — that is, by our single stupid selves and our acceptance of them

—but the end of the story is not the Cross but joy and an open gate into a new life.

✠   Lord, as we pray for grace to follow, help us to see also that you are a God who leads us.

Unending companionship
Ephesians 1:15-23

The Ascension of Christ is meaningless to us if we stop with the event itself. The pictures of the levitation of the risen Lord — of his rising into the sky — do us very ill service, if they cause us to concentrate on the outward, earthly happening. The real happening was that Christ's ministry as a man among us came to an end; that forever after his earthly incarnate presence was a memory to be cherished; and that what now opened to us was a new and unending companionship not limited by flesh and time, open to everyone, and leading directly to the presence of God in his fullness. In the passage from Ephesians, St. Paul prays that Christians may know the hope to which God calls us. That hope is nothing less than that we will accept the companionship he offers and live not as people who simply remember Galilee or as people who simply hope and wait for the future but as people who now, here, today, know and use the resources of power offered to us by the risen and ascended Lord.

✝ Lord Christ, Power of God, Wisdom of God, as you chose to be clothed in our flesh and so to raise it to immortality in your ascension, make us one with you in your victory and your glory.

Remembrance

At a Eucharist in the Cathedral at Kampala there were hundreds of Africans with their hands outstretched to receive the Bread. I could not communicate with them, for the language barrier lay between us. My life, my culture, my background were totally different from theirs. I was only too keenly aware of my limitations as a provincial Westerner, separated from them by a thousand factors over which I had little control.

Yet the unity of the Church was perfectly clear; and it was a unity established not by words or constitutions or formulas, but by Bread. This was the basis of the unity. As their hands reached forward to hold the Bread, so did mine; and somehow our differences began to disappear, in the enormous and wonderful and somehow frightening unity of the Bread. I don't know whether this remembrance can communicate to anybody else what it does to me. But I know that I shall never forget the way in which I was recalled to a true sense of the unity of Christ's body — the way in which the Church remembered its real nature — in that simple act.

But the deepest sense of remembrance is hidden in the act of God, and not of us at all. If Jesus were simply a good, dead man, then all the Lord's Supper could mean would be that we recalled the things He did and said, and corporately or individually rededicated ourselves to Him — to His memory, and to the trust of His teaching which we have inherited. I think it is fair to say that this is the meaning of the liturgy to many who share in it. It is an act of recollection — it is a little pageant re-enacted in order to stir within the worshippers a renewing and invigorating memory of one now long gone. It is an act by which we reach out of the now into the past, to re-establish in memory what once was true. I do not scorn that theology; I would feel that it was entirely true and helpful as far as it goes. But it does not go very far.

The point of the Christian religion is precisely that Christ is not a good, dead man, but that He reigns "at the right hand of God, in the glory of the Father."

It is a living Lord Whom we follow, not a dead hero. And this changes the whole character of eucharistic remembrance. It is far more a case of God remembering us than of our remembering Him. Our remembrance is simply a way to open a channel to God, and to claim His remembrance;

the important thing is that He meets us in our remembrance, in His own gracious presence and activity.

When God remembered His old Covenant with His people, then suddenly that Covenant became alive again — remembrance was the bringing into the present of what had been forgotten, had been relegated to the past. Just so is the remembrance of Him in the Holy Communion a doorway into the present, into the eternal.

Jesus is not a good, dead man. His love is not simply something to be remembered. It is an eternal fact about God. The Cross is not simply something that happened to Jesus of Nazareth 2000 years ago — it is a present description of God's love as it is. The ethical teaching of Jesus is not simply part of the biography of a great first-century teacher — it is the will of God now.

And remembrance is the act by which all this comes true, in the here and now. It isn't merely that because we remember it, therefore it becomes fresh in our minds. What happens is that our remembrance of it makes it possible for God's remembrance of us to take hold of us. Our memory is the gateway through which God enters, to re-establish His Covenant with us and open His love to us.

Where time and eternity meet

Eucharistic people take their lives, and break them, and give them, in daily fulfillment of what our Lord did and does. No need to ask what school of thought you follow or how you speculate about the manner of these things. He took His life in His own hands — this is Freedom. He broke it — this is Obedience. He gave it — this is Love. And He still does these simple acts at every altar and in every heart that will have it so; and Time and Eternity meet. The dying of the Lord Jesus and His life weave the wonderful, humble fabric of Christian discipleship.

Lake Champlain and the wedding garment

St. Matthew 22:1-14

Our Summer lake, like all well-brought-up lakes, has a sort of annual tide. In the Spring it is fat with the melting snow; but by midsummer, what with the heat and the exigencies of the local power system, it dwindles markedly, leaving a sort of high forehead of shore all around, and even an occasional island where once the fish marched and countermarched so solemnly.

What a difference it makes when the lake goes down! All sorts of things come to light — small sins once safely buried in the deep — cans riddled with an air rifle, a forbidden trolling-spoon which got caught-on-the bottom-and-the-string-broke honestly, a lost oarlock.

And how strange everything looks! The blue flag which used to mark the very furthest outpost of the land now rustles a score of feet from the water. Giant breakwaters and titanic wharves where our Lilliputian fleet used to do business, now what are they but little heaps of dry rocks far up on the beach? All the vast maritime enterprises of June by August are dusty and irrelevant anachronisms. The lake has gone down, and the great and splendid designs of the Summer's youth, and all its mistakes, are seen now for what they are.

It is hard not to see in this a parable of life. Time and tide alike have a way of uncovering our misdeeds — that is perhaps the most obvious lesson. But water that was once deep enough to fish in is not always so. And great rocks that once protected an anchorage of toy boats have a way of turning up as flat and disappointing cairns forgotten and half-buried in the sand. And by that token, the prayers of six are not safe prayers for sixty, nor the defenses of a boy adequate or relevant to a man.

"Friend, how camest thou in hither not having a wedding-garment?" That is the question the Gospel asks today; it is the question life asks every day. And suddenly dismayed, we look at our garments — our prayers, our rule of life, our old breakwaters against temptation, our postponed disciplines, our forgotten enterprises — and we see in truth that they belong to a time long-gone. There is a new shore line, (to come back to our fancy), and yesterday's hopes and plans will not work today.

If that were all, how unbearable life would be! We cannot answer the King's question; we do not know why we come without the wedding-garment; we do not even know that we have no wedding-garment. But the One who asks the question knows, before He asks. And He asks it so that we may know what He knows about ourselves, and that we may see that time does not wait, and that there is no safety for man anywhere in this life except in Him.

✟　A king made a supper and foolish men would not come and surly men came blind and graceless, not perceiving the immeasurable courtesy of the host. O King, renew in us the wedding garment of joy at Thy goodness in giving us life and the freedom to know and love and choose.

An Adventish thought

The problem of "putting Christ back into Christmas" is a lot more complicated than it seems. In the first place, I'm not clear that He ever left it, or ever fails to see us all with His grave and wonderful eyes, even when we are caught in the annual Yule rat-race. But more than that, it is precisely into this world that He comes, not into a gentle, pastoral economy of wondering shepherds and worshipping Kings. He knew all about it long before we did, and took account of the electric shavers, dish-washers, et al, as long ago as the Wilderness, when He said what He did about bread, and the glory of this world. As usual, He is a long way ahead of us; and at the moment, while it would be nice if everybody were a well-disciplined, middle-income Episcopalian (which is the net residue of "putting Christ back into Christmas" as far as I am concerned), I am more concerned with trying to learn to put Christmas, with all its brilliant squalor, back into His hands. I don't see anybody else who can manage it, frankly, and I can't imagine a more wonderful gift than this world, with its prodigious and imaginative skill, in the hands of the one Person who ever knew how to manage it.

Christmas 1946

We cannot wish you a Christmas half so joyful as the one already provided. We cannot wish for you a hope half so high as the reality already accomplished. We cannot wish for you a future half so bright as the life which day by day enfolds you. All we can wish you — and this we do with greatest enthusiasm — is eyes to see and ears to hear the real people (meaning most of all the Real Person) and a heart and will to love them (particularly Him), and the freedom to dream dreams which will do justice to reality.

Unto us is born this day

A cycle of hourly prayer for Christmastide
The cycle begins at eight o'clock p.m. on Christmas Eve

2000 · *As you have spoken it, so be it.* Your incarnation began in an act of obedience, O son of Mary; so is it to end *yet not what I will but what thou wilt.* Help us at this hour to find in your obedience the perfect freedom you were born to teach us, and we were born to learn.

St. Luke 1:38, St. Mark 14:36

2100 · Lord, we remember faithful Joseph who, not understanding, yet obeyed in patient and supporting love. We pray that such love — abiding, trusting, holding — may be given us by your goodness.

St. Matthew 1:24

2200 · *Being great with child,* she climbed the long hills to Bethlehem, weary, with Joseph by her side. Now at this hour, Lord, remember all in weariness and doubt, who hardly know who they are or where they are going, and let the light of Bethlehem show them what is hidden in your sure purposes and unfailing love.

St. Luke 2:4-5

2300 · There was no room for them and they went where they could, that God's will be done; and it was done. It is always so, O most unimagined and unexpected Lord, that what you choose to do is done; and it is done where we do not expect it or choose it; yet it is for our good that you turn even our ignorance and confusion to your purposes and your glory. Praise ever be to you, O unfailing Saviour.

St. Luke 2:7

Midnight · *All things were lying in peace and silence, and night in her swift course was half spent, when thy almighty Word leapt from thy royal throne in heaven into the midst of that doomed land like a relentless warrior, bearing the sharp sword of thy inflexible decree* . . . Hear us, O incarnate Word and Lord, and save us.

Wisdom of Solomon 18:14ff

0100 · The shepherds on their sleepy duty heard of you, O Lord Jesus, at this hour. Help me, wakeful and alone, to remember you afresh and the hope and light your coming gives me and all the world.

St. Luke 2:8-14

0200 · O Lord Jesus, whom Joseph took as in this night to seek shelter in Egypt, look in mercy on all refugees and homeless souls who have no place to lay themselves down in peace and take their rest. Grant them speedy help, and save us from hardness of heart.

St. Matthew 2:13-15

0300 · In the night Mary heard the shepherds tell of the angels and of Jesus, and she kept and pondered it in her heart. Lord, send this grace into my heart that I may think anew of your coming and wonder at it and rejoice that you came.

St. Luke 2:19

0400 · *The light shines on in the dark, O Lord, and the darkness has never mastered it.* Fill our hearts, I pray, with that light, that no darkness of this world may crush our hope and joy in following. The darkness has never mastered it! Thanks be to thee, the light.

St. John 1:5

0500 · Lord, if I wake now, let me remember *The night is far spent, the day is at hand* . . . let us walk honestly, as in the day. Help me to look ahead, not back at the night; to prepare for the honest walking of my life; to make ready for you who came as the light.

Romans 13:12-13

The first hour (0600) · Now ox and ass before him bow, that all may see how the whole creation knows itself and finds itself in you, and loves what it finds as best it can. Teach us, Lord, to be gentle and pitiful to all life, thankful for it, eager to use our power over it as a gift from you, content to learn from it about ourselves and claim true kinship with it that we may offer ourselves with all creation to you from whom we come.

St. Luke 2:7

0700 · The kings came, O Lord, bringing gifts to you as at this hour. Remember now, we pray, fathers and mothers, brothers, sisters, friends ... all who of their love have brought gifts to children and long that what they give may give love. Of your love, O child of Bethlehem, bless homes and families dear to us and dear to you.

St. Matthew 2:11

0800 · May the united, joyful love of the Holy Family at this hour shine in every family, to cleanse and deepen our love. May that same love cherish men and women who must be alone this day. May that same love open our eyes to all who are separated and unreconciled, and strengthen our will to make room for them in our hearts and lives.

The third hour (0900) · *The shepherds returned glorifying and praising God for what they had heard and seen.* Even so, Lord, help me not to be content with my own joy nor glad merely to remember Bethlehem, but turn my heart to praise you for what you have given us who are not wise enough to know what we needed nor good enough to ask for it, had we known.

St. Luke 2:20

1000 · *Among you, though you do not know him, stands the one . . .* The baby was unknown . . . but there is no harm in babies, and they are known and loved for what little they are. Father, help me to see him and know him, that there may be something of Bethlehem in every day and every meeting.

St. John 1:26

1100 · *Bethlehem in the land of Judah, you are far from the least in the eyes of the rulers of Judah.* The greatness of a city, O Lord, lies not in what it has but in what it hears. Guide our eyes away from what matters little to see what great souls you mean to make of the children who have nothing.

St. Matthew 2:6

The sixth hour (1200) · At this hour, when the sun is high, help us to remember him who was *the real light, which enlightens every man* ... not a lantern in the darkness but a blaze that makes every man, and manhood itself, inescapably clear, that casts the sharpest shadows, that opens every corner to our eyes. We may not ask you for the kindness of candlelight. In your light, there is nothing less than the truth. May we be strong enough to bear it.

St. John 1:9

The seventh hour (1300) · *God sent his own son, born of a woman, born under the law.* Like to us, bone of our bone, you sent him, O Father, that we might know what you think of us and that you might know what it is like to be us, and that we both might meet in him. May it be so, every day of our life.

Galatians 4:4

1400 · As at this hour, men came at the king's will to kill the babies, that the King of Kings might surely not live to reign; but it was not his time to die. In mercy, Father, guard and keep all who suffer for what they are not or for the accidents of blood or color or creed or tongue; and teach us to remember them, and remember him who chose his own time to reign and die.

St. Matthew 2:16

The ninth hour (1500) · *He hath shewed strength with his arm; he hath scattered the proud in the imagination of their hearts.* The proud do not imagine a man-child. Now, as then, in our pride we are scattered to the hopelessness of our own strength and the loneliness of our own devices; now, as then, you do what you mean to do in your own way. Teach us to imagine your things and accept your unconquerable strength.

St. Luke 1:51

The tenth hour (1600) · It is still light enough to see; even a baby in a cellar-hole could be seen; but the night also comes when it is hard to see. In that night, O Lord, we rejoice that *your righteousness hath been openly shewed in the sight of the heathen.* He is sure, thanks be to God.

Psalm 98:2

The eleventh hour (1700) · *He hath in these last days spoken unto us by his son.* When there first were Christians, they could still remember the son who was born, who spoke, in these last days. The days are not changed, nor is your voice, O Lord. Help us to hear and remember you, for it was not so long ago.

Hebrews 1:2

1800 · Let this day come to its close in joy, as it began, O Lord. Let our supper be blessed, and our play and our sleep, as all our days are blessed because you chose to make them yours.

1900 · *Lord, now lettest thou thy servant depart in peace ... for mine eyes have seen thy salvation.* May your peace in the night season be ours, because we know what you have done and will unfailingly do, and our hearts may be serene and our purposes sure and our courage high.

St. Luke 2:29-30

January

January, I have long felt, is a month without which life would be greatly improved. Annual reports, final days of reckoning with postponed business, new budgets, clearing out of files . . . to say nothing of Christmas bills and the like . . . it is a miserable, harassed, snivelling, crass, over-bearing, worldly wretch of a month.

Sublime irrelevance
St. Mark 9:7

There is a sublime irrelevance in Christ-Jesus to what is going on. This is what wins us to Him and frightens us about Him. It is not what helps us to understand Him, because we cannot fit Him into that, we cannot fit Him into any of our categories. He comes on His own terms. He is God's idea of what it is to be a man, and He is that in His way, the way of the Cross, the way of Love, the way of Passion, the way of Pain, the way of sacrifice, the way of heroism, the way of loneliness, the way of joy, the way of sadness, the way of death, the way of beauty, the way of truth. He abides in His way, and on His terms, and He will not be captured. "This is my beloved Son. Hear Him!" This is where we start and indeed, this is where any deep understanding of the ways of God must start — on God's terms, not ours.

✠   Lord, keep us steadfast in our commitment to you.

The virtue of imagination
St. Matthew 25:31-46

We hope you saw the moving little story in last Sunday's newspapers — about the Irish poet who needed bananas in his sickness and there were no bananas to be had in Ireland so they cabled Mayor O'Dwyer and he found some and sent them with a policeman to the first plane and over they went.

Maybe we are more mawkish than we usually are, what with a rainy Monday and all, but at all events we have decided that this banana deal is about the best use the cable or the trans-Atlantic airplane has been put to in some time, and that it wouldn't hurt us any if we thought more about the need of one man for some food rather than the "estimated requirement of the Ruritanian populace of 393,471 long tons of cereal grains during the next eight months" (by which we mean that the R. p. breaks down into thousands of people who need things to live).

The truth is, isn't it, that there is an enormous difference between one, sick, Irish poet and the hordes of anonymous Ruritanians? It is a classic difficulty, mentioned by a first-century King in St. Matthew 25:31-46, a passage to which we invite your attention. It is the central difficulty of our society. And the point we keep coming back to, in our reflections, is that God gave us imaginations for just such difficulties as these, and that our trouble is we are so busy counting the vast numbers and being impressed by them that we never have time to sit down and think about any one of them.

"Be still, then, and know that I am God," or, if we may change it a little, "Be still, then, and know that this man is your brother." We invite your attention again, this time to the present tense — "this man is your brother." That is the imaginative tense, in this case. Even the callous ones in the parable of the sheep and the goats would have agreed in saying "should be." But it is the direct and joyous virtue of the imagination to go beyond what ought to be to what is.

✠   Lead me to be merciful this day, to minister to the least of Thy brethren and remember that so we may minister to Thee, O Mighty Lord, hungry, thirsty, a stranger, naked, sick, in prison.

A new reality

What is the Nation or the Church or the family, for that matter, except the empty space between separate selves and separate places until, one by one, the filaments of our common life, our sense of obligation, of partnership, are spun across the distance, and the emptiness is crossed and a new reality appears?

Our alms of time
St. Matthew 2:10-11

Our eyes happened to fall, the other day, on a gentleman's hands performing a very simple office — specifically he was carefully removing a cigar band to adorn the finger of his tiny grand-daughter. It took some little time to extricate the paper jewel and make a suitable presentation, time enough for a fugitive observation on our part which seemed to us to have some bearing on life and on the Epiphany.

The thought that came to us was, first, a wisp of wonder at the gentleness and patience of a busy man, through whose hands there passed great affairs, who yet found the time to deal carefully and lovingly with a little child. It is not unheard of, we know, for men to be so kind, yet it never fails to move us and even chide us a bit. But more than that, our mind moved on to consider how little time a person has, really, in the swift-moving years, and how tempted we are to be too mindful of that.

We are beguiled into being misers of time — too important for this, too careful for that, too impressed with the many demands and the few hours — and often, in the end, look back with

sadness and wish we had been a little more care-
less, a little less cautious.

There isn't much time, that's the truth. But do
you really have to be quite so busy? These thirty
seconds, these thirty years are an appreciable and
important part of your life. You can measure
them, and you must spend them wisely. They are
all the time you have. But do you really have to
be quite so efficient? Maybe, as with a gentleman
and his granddaughter, it is better to take a lot of
time with a cigar ring and be remembered for
that. Maybe tomorrow you will be glad you did.
Maybe the Maker of Time can catch up the slack
so you won't have to worry too much about
whether you spent each minute or each year in
the most carefully rationalized way.

Those "maybes" are real: we do not pretend that
all this is more than a sentimental and fleeting
question. But the value of the Gifts at
Bethlehem, and the value of what this next hour
or year or decade may be, strike us as two aspects
of the same question. And as He accepted those
tinsel gifts, so He may, (and so may He) accept
our simple, generous, affectionate alms of time.

✛ O Loving Father, help us to bear each
other's burdens and to study each other's needs;
and vouchsafe to Thy people who wait upon
Thee, clearer vision, deeper understanding, and
the strength to obey.

Our daily course
A cycle of prayer beginning at 12 pm

Midnight · Thou Who with Thine own mouth didst teach that at midnight the Bridegroom shall come, grant that the cry The Bridegroom Cometh may sound evermore in our ears, that so we be never unprepared to meet Him; and save us.

Andrewes

0100 · Thou Who for us men and our salvation wast born at dead of night, give us daily to be born again by renewing of the Holy Ghost, till Thou be formed anew in us unto a perfect man; and save us.

Andrewes

0200 · Jesus Who dost still as ever watch over all Thy children and bless them, bless those who also watch and wait, and in the dark come quickly to give what we know not how to ask; and save us.

0300 · Lord Jesus Who didst rise up a great while before day and pray alone for those who slept, be with us who cannot sleep, and help us to pray for those who cannot pray.

St. Mark 1:35

0400 · Thou, Lord, art in the midst of us and we are called by Thy name. Help us remember Thee Who slept in the boat while they feared the storm, and how Thou didst wake to rebuke it; and give us whose courage fails the steadiness we need. Hold us close to Thee; and save us.

St. Matthew 8:23-27

0500 · Blessed Lord Who before the dawn didst rise from death to bring us life, help us to rejoice that you are, and you reign, and you do not fail. Give us thankful and bold spirits, Lord; and save us.

The first hour (0600) · Thou Who in early light didst bid weary Simon let down his net for a draft, renew our obedience and our trust, that this day may be offered Thee in faith, and its harvest richer than we dare hope.

St. Luke 5:4-11

0700 · O Pitiful Lord, remember Judas, amazed and broken by his sin, who in the morning cast down the money and went and hanged himself; and remember all who have betrayed Thee and do not know Thy mighty power to make whole again and to forgive; and save us.

St. Matthew 27:3-10

0800 · Let us be, O Lord, as those who at this hour go on watch, to offer our duties and our hours to Thee this day. May we be content to do what this day holds, eat this day's bread, do this day's tasks, and put all into Thy hands with a single mind.

The third hour (0900) · Thou Who at the third hour didst send down Thy Holy Ghost on the Apostles: Take not away Thy Holy Spirit from us, but renew Him daily within us; and save us.

Andrewes

1000 · At this hour, O Lord, Thou didst call and send Simon and Andrew to be fishers of men. Teach me daily to hear that call, for it is mine, too, and remember it and obey it.

1100 · O Lord Jesus, Who at this hour was mocked on the Cross, steady me with Thy sure peace and hold me true with Thy constancy, that I may not forget Thee nor fail myself for whom Thou didst suffer the Cross.

The sixth hour (1200) · Almighty Savior Who at midday didst call Thy servant St. Paul to be an apostle to the Gentiles, we beseech Thee to illuminate the world with the radiance of Thy glory that all nations may come and worship Thee.

The seventh hour (1300) · Thou Who at the seventh hour didst will that the fever leave the nobleman's son; if aught abide of fever or sickness in our soul, take it from us also. Watch with us, we pray, over all who are sick and all who minister to them, and do for them and in them what we are not wise enough nor good enough to ask.

Andrewes, Adapted

1400 · Lord Jesus, Who didst feed the multitude with what in our eyes seems so little, teach us to be mindful of Thy power more than our weakness, and to seek ever to put what little we have into Thy hands to bless and multiply and use for others' needs.

The ninth hour (1500) · O Lord Jesus Christ Who at this hour didst die upon the Cross, holding out Thine arms in love and pity for all men everywhere, grant that all men may look unto Thee and be saved.

The tenth hour (1600) · Thou Who at the tenth hour didst will Thine apostles, whenas they found Thy Son, to declare with great joy We have found the Messias; make us also like sort to find the Messias, and when He is found, in like sort to rejoice; and save us.

Andrewes

The eleventh hour (1700) · Thou Who didst vouchsafe even at the eleventh hour to send men into Thy vineyard and to fix a wage, notwithstanding they had stood all the day idle; Do unto us like favor and though it be late, as it were about the eleventh hour, accept us graciously when we return to Thee; and save us.

Andrewes

1800 · Thou Who at the hour of supper didst will to institute the most sacred mysteries of Thy Body and Blood; make us mindful of the same and partakers thereof, and that, never unto judgment but unto remission of sin and unto acquiring of the bequests of the new testament; and save us.

Andrewes

1900 · When the sun was setting, they brought the sick to Jesus; and He laid His hands on every one of them and healed them. Look in mercy now, Lord, on all who are sick and all who minister to them and all who love them. Help us to remember that whatever man does or does not do, Thou art always the same and failest not.

St. Mark 1:32

2000 · Lord Jesus, Who at this hour didst say to those at table with Thee *He that is greatest among you, let him be as the younger, and he that is chief as he that doth serve;* wherever my place, let it be an altar; whatever I am called to be or do, let it be an offering to Thy glory and Thy love.

St. Luke 22:26

2100 · Jesus Who at this time didst appear transfigured before Thy sleepy disciples, wake me and cleanse my eyes to see Thee in those around me, and hear the Father's voice that Thou art His Son, and hear Him and hear Thee, and see them in Thee and in Him.

St. Luke 9:28-36

2200 · When few could see, the righteous Nicodemus came to find what manner of man Christ was, and for his pains was not comforted but heard he must be born again. So let us now not be at ease in Zion, but hear Thy word and not fear the new birth but seek it.

St. John 3:1

2300 · The disciples toiled at their rowing, for the wind in the night, and feared lest this night it be too strong. But Thou didst come, walking, to say Be of Good Cheer. Lord, come to say this to us, when we are afraid the storm is greater than we or Thee, and warm our hearts and make us glad we are alive.

St. Mark 6:50

Reminders of wilderness
St. Matthew 4:1-11

One of the city-dweller's few consolations is the occasional intrusion of nature in the raw, to remind him that bricks and mortar are not the only real things. We found a nest with some eggs in it a while ago, tucked into a most unlikely corner of a public building ... we watched a squirrel the other morning, nibbling and crunching speculatively on a piece of ice ... just outside our window there has been a lumber operation going on, including cutting the tree down, and sawing it up into cordwood ... very minor events, indeed, but well-calculated to remind us, as *rus in urbe* ever does, that there is a wild world just outside the door of civilization, closer and more insistent than we remember.

Of course, it is a rather sophisticated *rus* in our *urbe*. The fledgelings from the nest will, in due time, be swearing out of the corners of their mouths at the cops and taxis. The squirrel beyond question is as tough a little guttersnipe as his brothers are in these parts: we could almost hear him damning the sharpies who took him on that ice deal — you can't trust anybody in this joint. Even the lumbering was a pale laboratory experiment — no "Timber-r-r-r," no calking irons, no

Spring drive — the thing came down scientifically in sections like an Erector set, with the most exaggerated reverence for the School of Mines; and the local Paul Bunyans (Royal Foresters in King's College days, no doubt) didn't even chew tobacco.

But *rus* it still is, thanks to the merciful God of nature who needles us periodically with such reminders that we weren't born with shoes on, that a cornered man looks exactly like a cornered rat from the endocrine point of view, that those strong weeds, lust and fear, will grow as easily in a city lot as anywhere else, that domestication is as hard for a man as it is for a tiger — even harder, because we have two homes in which to learn how to live.

Civilization is pretty thin ice, and fragile. It is a good thing that we be reminded of that and of the wilderness just outside the door of our house. It is a good thing to start thinking about His forty days in the wilderness. It is a good thing to remember what St. Paul said, "I keep under my body, and bring it into subjection . . ."

✝   We see you, Lord, in the midst of our struggle. Help us to see ourselves, and find ourselves, in you.

Exploring outer space
Col. 1:15-20

Looking recently at televised pictures of the moon taken by the Ranger cameras, I grew reflective about how easy it is to take such extraordinary technical accomplishments for granted. It did not seem extraordinary at the start, to think of this celestial taxicab racing across the lunar landscape, throwing pictures out the window, but halfway through the broadcast, there was suddenly for me a psychological crash. It hit me that I was being tempted by precisely the innocent blasphemy of the people of our times who take such gifts for granted. We do not know — we do not remember — how long God has waited until He could teach us these skills. We forget the wonderful ingenuity and the patient love of God who over the milleniums worked and worked with His creation until there could be this kind of response. So quickly have we taken our scientific feats for granted; so quickly, we are ready to move on to other and newer frontiers.

It is a perilous moment for mankind when we take any knowledge for granted, when at any time the miraculous transaction of teaching and learning ever is taken for granted as part of the normal structure, the normal housekeeping of life. It should never be. The miracle of existence, the miracle of exploration, the miracle of learning, the miracle of teaching — these are the perennial intimations of God.

✠ "O Lord God Almighty, who savest our life from destruction and crownest us with mercy and loving-kindness, we yield thee humble and hearty thanks for the great hope lately given us and all thy children. All truth is thine and of thine own does our healing come. Accept, O Lord, from grateful hearts the praise for what intent and faithful men have learned; Teach us to use this truth with humility and courtesy; And, of thy mercy, grant that as new hope of life comes to us in the shadow of death, so we may also walk soberly, not forgetting that this mortal must put on immortality. Hear our prayer and receive our prayer, O Pitying God, through the merits and mediation of Him through whom all healing comes, our Lord Jesus Christ, who with thee and the Holy Spirit livest and reignest God, forever and ever."

Moments on the road of choice
Genesis 1:26-27

It is a very perilous road, the road of choice. It is an agonizing road. It is filled with obstacles and pain, for others as well as ourselves. But it has its moments — it has its moments when, for the first time, the glory and the dignity of the human animal is clear, at least for a moment, in a flash. Mankind rises to reclaim the image of God which was on him at the beginning and yet which is never safely his. He rises to claim it; and in these moments in human experience — moments of greatness, moments of pity, moments of courage, moments of integrity, moments of truth — these are the moments when the mark of God on man is clearest and sharpest.

Whatever the mark of God was upon us in the Garden of Eden, whatever the mark of God was like in the beginning when He first made us in our innocence and put His mark on us, we shall never know, because that mark we have lost. But in the tumult and the battle and the pain and the grime and the sweat of life, there do come great moments.

✝ Lord Jesus, you show us what we really are; help us to become what we are.

The mark of the wounds

Jesus said, "I am known of mine." But when you apply this to God and ask the question "Does God say that I know Him?" then we are incredulous. What can anyone know about God in Himself? What possible description can we give of God? We understand full well that even the greatest words we have in our theological vocabularies or whatever are simply symbolic words that refer to something that you cannot describe. There is no name for God. There is no way to "talk about Him." There are simply signposts toward Him. He is like a father, He is like love, He is like strength, He is like honor; but what He is no man can know.

And yet the preposterous, ridiculous Christian faith says: "No, there is more here that must be said. You do know God. You do know Him — in the wounds." How often in the resurrection stories at Eastertide we are recalled to this. When the hidden, risen Christ comes among the disciples, their eyes are held, they do not know him, He is a mystery, until in some way or another, as to Thomas, He says, "Look at the wounds in the hands, in the feet, in the side; see that it is I. No specter ... no dream ... no vision ... see the wounds so that you will know that it is I." The Church can never forget this. We know God by His wounds. We may not know what He is in Himself but we know the wounds.

"Where will I find God at work in all of this tumult and turmoil — where is He?" Ask of our society "Where does it hurt? Where are people hungry? Where are they fighting a crushing injustice?" There — wherever there is need and pain and the fight for justice — you know that you will find Christ. He will be elsewhere too, no doubt; but He will be there, because those who hurt are His, and He is there with them in their sorrow and their aches and their deprivation. He is with the poor. He is with those who are struggling to establish a fairer justice in this world. This is a way you have of knowing Him, because you go where you know He is.

There is no preaching of the Christian gospel, and there is no living of the Christian life, and there is no true witness of the Church in society which does not have wounds.

The Day of the Passion

1800 · The woman broke the box for good and all; and it was for good because she willed to lose forever what was hers that she might share His death and He be praised. So help us Lord to share Thy passion, not idly as those who watch and go away, but as people who will to break and lose what has been dear to us, that we may have part with Thee.

St. Mark 14:3

1900 · As they ate, He took bread and brake it, and gave unto them, saying, This is my body . . . Blessed Lord, it was now that Thou didst break this bread, and now that I pray to call to mind and do again what Thou didst do. Help me to make of my daily bread a thankful remembrance, and of my life an offering with Thee and for Thee.

St. Luke 22:19

2000 · Now at this hour Jesus knelt to wash their feet, that they might somehow break through pride and propriety to know the love that was to be shown to all the world. Wherever I am, help me, O unfailing Lord, to remember the needs of others and love them, as Thou dost love them and me.

St. John 13:5

2100 · Now, Lord, Thou didst go forth with those whom Thou didst love, singing the songs of Zion for what they thought was past but Thou knew still lay ahead; Teach me to give thanks for all Thou hast done and yet will do; and clothe my spirit with thanksgiving for Gethsemane and the choice at this hour made for me.

St. Mark 14:26

2200 · Though I should die with Thee, said Peter, I will not deny Thee; and so said they all and we all. Yet he and they and we have need of more than our own strength if we are to be true. O Pitiful Lord, who knows our need before we ask and our shame of asking, save us from a greater shame and give us what is Thy will and not our deserving.

St. Mark 14:31

2300 · O Lord Jesus, Who didst pray alone and choose alone; help us to remember Thy lonely, steadfast love, and rejoice in it, and seek to share it, and build our lives around it.

St. Luke 22:42

Midnight · O Saviour of the world, Who at this hour was led away to the High Priest to face a darkness more black than any dark; keep us faithful in our witness for you in word and deed; and save us.

St. Mark 14:53

0100 · O Saviour of the world, Who at this hour heard false witness and kept your peace, help me abide content in the truth, and brave and wise in my silence as well as my words.

St. Matthew 26:63

0200 · You held your peace and would not give the answers which would save Your life. But when the high priest sought the answer on which our life depends, You said I Am, and saved us. Teach us, confused, how to tell the important from the unimportant, the selfless from the self-regarding, and save us anew this night.

St. Mark 14:60-62

0300 · You were still, Jesus, when they blindfolded you and hit you and dared you say who did strike you. You did not say It was My Brother; but it was he; and it was for him You were to die. O Hidden Brother, open my eyes.

St. Mark 14:65

0400 · At cockcrow, O Lord, Peter remembered his vain promise, and knew that you knew, and turned his face away and wept. Help me, O Saviour of the World, not to boast of my faith and my works; if I boast, help me to remember Peter; if I remember, help me to know that You know; if I know, help me not just to weep but to accept your knowing with penitence and joy; and save us.

St. Luke 22:60-61

0500 · O Saviour, help me remember Judas and his whirling helplessness at this hour, before light, when he was sure you were lost, and the Kingdom would not be taken by storm. Cleanse my heart to know more truly that all things are safe with you, and your hand cannot be forced. Help us to abide in patience and humbleness of heart, to wait in hope, to share your pain, to receive your love; and save us.

St. Matthew 27:3-5

The first hour (0600) · Now at this time Pilate sat and wondered at the silent Man, and then, unbelieving and content with a small duty, washed his hands of Jesus. O Saviour, take from us the fear of great possibilities and keep us from safe unbelief. Cleanse us so we can see you where you stand and hear you, though unspeaking, and follow you, now and here.

St. Matthew 27:24

0700 · The soldiers played King as with a fool, and Thou didst suffer them, for Thou art no fool's King but another kind yet to be known. Thou didst suffer, and suffer them, and wait. Keep us from their folly, O King of all Creation, and help us know what it is to be ruled by Thy love and Thy holiness.

St. Matthew 27:27-30

0800 · Along the dolorous way Thou didst walk, but as a conqueror, bidding the world look to its sorrows, not to Thine. Teach us anew to see Thy strength and Thy constancy in the midst of this world's ceaseless grasping talk, and help me pass this day in quietness and with a tranquil mind.

St. Luke 25:26-32

The third hour (0900) · Now they crucified my Lord; now they nailed Him to the Tree. So each day begins, remembering the wood and the nails. So let it ever be that each day's work be blessed with a real choice and a real death, that it be a fit offering to add to Thine.

St. Luke 23:33

1000 · Lord, even as they lifted Thee on the Cross, Thou didst lift them to the Father's throne, praying that He forgive their unknowing sin. May it be with us that no grief nor pain may hide from us the love from which no secrets are hid, which knows our need before we ask and our ignorance in asking, which takes and uses us just as we are, and when, and where.

St. Luke 23:34

1100 · Lord, Thou, in the midst of Thy Passion, didst yet find room in Thy heart for Mary and John, and provide for them. So save us from the monstrous selfishness of pain, that in our deepest woe we yet may turn our eyes away from ourselves to those whom Thou dost also love.

St. John 19:25-27

The sixth hour (1200) · As if the world could not bear to see what was happening, the dark descended on the Cross at noonday. Yet the saving offering went on, and does go on, in every darkness. Hold us steady in the dark brightness of this life, O Saviour, that we may never forget Thy ceaseless, secret work.

St. Matthew 27:45

1300 · You said I Thirst, and meant no more than a child means, waking in the night, or a man means as he works and sweats. Even here, even on this final altar, it was our thirsting flesh and blood that was being raised to glory. Help us be glad that we are men and women, loved in this flesh, called to Thee in this flesh; and save us.

St. John 19:28

1400 · You said It Is Finished when the world could see it was hardly begun. Yet you were right: No man has much time; no age has much liberty; we must take things in time and gather what is ready; and in the Father's hands, Who has all time, all things are made whole. Teach us to seek our duties and do them, and then rest in peace.

St. John 19:30

The ninth hour (1500) · He cried with a loud voice, as we cry that others may know, that God may know we are alone and at the end of everything we can do. At that hour, O unfailing Father, Thou didst hear and take Him to life. Even so, teach us not to lose hope but to cry out, without fear, knowing that Thou art sure.

St. Mark 15:37

The tenth hour (1600) · The soldier said Truly this Man was the Son of God, not knowing what he meant but only that he must say the highest words to match this Man and mark His death. No words could truly speak for him, nor can they for us. We know not what we say. Hear Thou our praise and thanksgiving through our stumbling sounds, and grant us the joy of loving Thee, however foolishly, and worshipping Thee, whatever fault there be in what we say.

St. Mark 15:39

The eleventh hour (1700) · Thou Who at eventide didst will to be taken down from the cross and buried in a tomb; Take away our sins from us and bury them in Thy sepulchre, covering with good works whatsoever we have committed ill; and save us.

Andrewes

The true antithesis

... we are beguiled into sentimentality when we adjudge the secular world as a 'materialist' world and long for a more 'spiritual' quality of life. Christianity is not a particularly spiritual religion; in fact it is rather suspicious of spirituality; it is a sacramental religion, very down-to-earth, very materialistic when it deals with the material, very aware of the fallen angels, very aware that the Devil is also a spirit.

The antithesis to the secular, industrial society is not a clerical, ethical society, where prayer and art will take the place of machines and plants. The true antithesis is between a society that has no God to whom it may offer its handiwork, and a society to which the act of oblation is the final and concluding act of the whole inventive process.

✠   Let this day, O Lord, be my servant and let me be thine, that when the evening comes I may be free to offer thee a finished and a peaceful task, seen clearly in the morning light, and done in quiet and unhurried purpose.

A parable, like a star shell, is expected to go off and give a light for a little while so we can get our bearings. It is like the lance which kills a whale — it slices painlessly and unnoticed through the blubber, and then the explosive head detonates to the fatal discomfiture of the whale. But the lance was not intended to tell the whale where to swim next. The Pharisees and scribes got precious few rules for daily living from the story of the lost sheep . . .

A dial of parables

This cycle starts at 7 o'clock in the morning.

0700 · O Lord, as Thou didst teach the disciples to mind red sky at morning and so remember to read the signs of the times, so at this hour teach me to read the face of humanity and see the world I live in, that I may know Thy will and Thy love and Thy pain and Thy glory this day.

St. Matthew 16:3-4

0800 · Help me to build this day on Thee, O Lord, like a man building a house on rock, that I may be sure and steady in what I do for Thee and not shaken from my duty for fear of Thine enemies.

St. Luke 6:46-49

The third hour (0900) · Lead me to be merciful this day, to minister to the least of Thy brethren and remember that so we minister to Thee, O Mighty Lord, hungry, thirsty, a stranger, naked, sick, in prison.

St. Matthew 25:31-46

1000 · O Master, help me to plan wisely and be the master of my time, that I may count the cost of the tower of this day's work for Thee and try not to do more than I can or less than I ought.

St. Luke 14:25-33

1100 · Sparrows go for ten a penny in the market, He said, and yet not one is forgotten in God's eyes. Help me then, O my Friend, to remember that I am not nameless before the Father, nor is anyone; and He is well able to know me and love me as I am.

St. Luke 12:6-7

The sixth hour (1200) · When the sun was up, the seed was scorched, and because it had no root it withered away. Lord, help me now to lift mine eyes and see what Thou hast sown this day, and turn my hands to tend those seeds lest they die.

St. Matthew 4:3-13

1300 · O Merciful God, burn away my pride that I may remember my great debt and all Thou hast forgiven me, and remember my cold heart, and change me that I may wash Thy feet with my tears and love Thee more and be saved.

St. Luke 7:36-50

1400 · Thou didst say If a house be divided against itself, it cannot stand. My house is divided; I serve two masters; I bargain to gain a place in two worlds; I am not able to choose one Lord and one self. Lord, give me the grace to desire and seek a single heart.

St. Mark 3:22-29

The ninth hour (1500) · At this hour when the sun is still high, we remember how the man lay bare and broken, and how the Samaritan saw not a body but a brother, not a balance but a duty. Save us from quick coldness of heart or cheap turning away, and help us see Thee, the Victim, in every hurt soul, and Thee, the Stranger, in every act of love.

St. Luke 10:25-37

The tenth hour (1600) · Now is the Pharisee's time, of adding up the day's work to make mention to Thee that we are not as other men are, that we have given tithes of all we possess. Save us, O Vigilant Lord, from the fear that unless we pull Thy sleeve we shall be ignored, and grant us the splendid confidence to know we are loved and need not try to buy what is already given.

St. Luke 18:9-14

The eleventh hour (1700) · At this hour the Prodigal came home, holding on his tongue the words that seemed right to say, not knowing that his father had long seen him, and had a greater thing for him than any remorse could win. Let me come home, my Lord, this hour and every hour, to find what I scarce believe exists, yet know must unimaginably be true if even earthly fathers are like this.

St. Luke 15:11-32

1800 · Lord, look in gentleness on us, men and women, considering our bodies, what we shall put on, and give us simplicity of heart this night. O Master of all Beauty, teach us that the Father knows we have need of all these things, and help us to trust more in being what we are.

St. Matthew 6:28-34

Midnight · Jesus, Lord, Who told us of the friend who came at midnight to ask bread of his friend, teach us and help us to let no weariness or worry of our own keep us from hearing what is really asked of us and giving what is really needed.

St. Luke 11:5-13

0100 · Jesus, Lord, Who taught us to be like men who wait for their lord that they may open unto him immediately, keep us ready at all times to hear your step, know your voice, and open the door of our heart to you.

St. Luke 12:36

0200 · The Kingdom is like a seed sown by a man, and he sows and sleeps and wakes and sleeps again, and knows not how the sleepless seed springs up and grows. So is it in the sleep of our souls as of our bodies, that God still gives His seed its own life and teaches it to grow and prepares a harvest, all unbeknownst to us. Teach me this, Lord, that I may sleep in peace.

St. Mark 4:26-29

0300 · I light my lamp not that I may see the lamp or see myself, but that I may see the room and what is in it and how big it is and that I am at peace. So may it be, Lord, with my faith, that it may light the world that others may see the world and what is in it and how big it is, and so be at peace.

St. Matthew 5:14-16

The Pharisee and the Publican
St. Luke 18:9-14

Wthat was the difference between them? What was the sin of the Pharisee? We come to this point, and we wrestle with it, in one way or another until we see what the sin of the Pharisee was. It was, surely, that the Pharisee was his own judge, that he was playing God for himself, that he had already passed judgment on himself and it was a favorable judgment, that he was content with what he had done. And because he was playing God — because he was, for the moment, God, saying I thank myself that I am not as other men are — for that moment, at any rate, God could not do anything for him. He was his own god, and he was stuck with himself. The publican, for the moment, had the grace to know that he wasn't any god at all and had no god with which to console himself; and therefore God could, for the moment, do something for him.

We do get to the point where we can see that far into the parable. It is a disturbing parable, but we accept that. Of course, our first reaction is one of tremendous gratitude that we have seen these two types, and can say before God, "Thank God I am not as that Pharisee is." And then there is an uncomfortable silence: then, thirty seconds later, we come to ourselves, and we say, "Well, that was certainly asinine. Here I fell right into the same trap. How grateful I am that I have discovered this. I thank God that I am not like that publican who thought he wasn't a Pharisee and was a Pharisee because he thought he wasn't a Pharisee." And so it goes.

It's like trying to catch your finger, of course. You never can quite catch it. First you're proud; and then you are ashamed and humble because you were proud; and then you are proud because you were so humble when you discovered how proud you had been . . . .

And it goes on, this damned cycle of sin. This is pride. This is what pride means — I've got to be my own god, I have got to be right, I have got to judge myself, I have got to be better than other men are, I have got to know that I am either the best person that ever lived or the worst person that ever lived (and there really isn't much difference between these two). We cannot stand being in the middle. We've got to be better than our neighbors, or worse, or somehow unique. We've got to be better than the Pharisee or the publican or whatever, or else, we've got to be much worse, so that we can be better because we are worse and know we are worse . . . .

This is the human predicament, this eternal self-consciousness before God. It is absolutely universal. There is no way in which you can pull yourselves up by your own boot straps spiritually. There is no way in which you can be your own judge. There is no way in which you can be God. The only possible way of sanity is being willing to receive from God what you cannot buy. You cannot earn this. You cannot be good enough or bad enough to deserve God's attention. The final humiliation of the human spirit is in accepting the fact that God knows what we are like and loves us as we are. And if you get to that point by the time you die, you're lucky.

The Bible

... the Bible probably wasn't written to provide
an enjoyable aesthetic experience for the literate.
God had a greater purpose, I do not doubt, than
to supply good English prose. Certainly the Bible
should scare the wits out of us rather than please
us by its antique gentility.

What it is to be human

God makes us what we are, as we are and therefore He knows our weaknesses and He knows our possibilities. He knows what we were made to be; He knows the farthest limits of the range of the human spirit; therefore God expects great things from us. This disturbs us sometimes when intimations of it come to us. We do not feel ourselves to be very great. We are not very strong. We are not very wise. God knows we are not very good. And when in life we encounter the choices that demand great response from us, our first answer is likely to be one of fear. Men were not meant to walk like kings this way. We were not meant to be strong like this. We want to retreat into comfortable mediocrity, where there is safety in numbers. But God is not content with this, because He knows what it is to be human. He made us — indeed in Christ He came inside our humanity and knows it ... the texture of it ... the touch of it ... the sweetness of it ... the ache of it ... the pain of it ... from inside. "I know my sheep." And therefore He continues to expect as well as understand.

There is only one ministry

The most urgent truth about the Church is what is hidden in our fumbling phrase, "the ministry of the laity." It is not a phrase I like very much, for it suggests that there are many ministries, and this is really not true. There is only one ministry — Christ's ministry. He is the only Minister there is in the Church. It is He Who receives the baby into His great Body in baptism; it is He Who puts His hands over mine in confirmation or ordination; it is He Who stands at the altar and breaks the Bread. He is the Bishop and Shepherd of our souls; He is the great High Priest Who has passed into the heavens; He is the Lamb Who offered His life, wholly and completely, and showed us what it is to be free. There is no way of chopping up His ministry and giving bits of it to one or to another.

Because Christ is One and there is only one ministry, then priest and layman alike need to learn that their separate lives are only two sides of the same coin — that the great imperatives of the Gospel lie over both — that both together must fulfill the work of Christ in this world.

God at work

The mission is God's, not ours. He is the One who is at work out there. We go out to meet Him. We go out to encounter our blessed Lord, creating and sustaining and loving and forgiving and inspiring and dying and being born again even among the people of the world who do not know His name, who would even spit His name out of their mouths.

The pain and the search and the torment and the itch of a new society being born is God at work. The new knowledge that flickers and flames into fire in these societies is His. And such grace and wisdom as men come to know it, is His. He is at work there and the mission of redeeming and fulfilling is His.

And to us, less than the least of all saints, is this grace given that we are privileged to go where He is and for a minute to stand by His side.

Mysteries and splendors

I tell you, my friends, that the glory and the holiness of being a man is like nothing else under the sun. I don't mean a "great man" (for every man is great) nor a "good man" (for God has made every man good). I mean just being human. The fact of being free and responsible — the fact that man's nature is always in peril of being less than it is and always capable of being more — the fact that he can think and love and dream and pity and imagine and build and bear pain and bear glory — the fact that God made us, and loves us enough to fulfill and complete our humanity from inside — these are the eternal mysteries and splendors of life. Whether we are willing to live up to the holiness God gave us is our problem. But the holiness is no problem. It is there for every man to see.

Christ is the true size of us, and the truth about us. And every one of us, in our heart of hearts, hopes that humanity can take this truth, and live up to it.

O God, we ask Thee not to lift us out of life but to prove Thy power within it.

We ask not for tasks more suited to our strength but for strength adequate to our tasks. Give us the vision that inspires and the grace that endures. Save us from the sin of futile sorrow which only sees but does not act. Stir up our wills to practice that brotherhood by which alone the Kingdom of The Christ is wrought upon the earth. And give us, we pray, the grace of Jesus Christ Who wore our flesh like a king's robe, Who walked the ways of earth like a conqueror in triumph, and Who now lives and reigns with Thee in the unity of the same spirit, ever one God, world without end.

Amen.

Stephen Fielding Bayne, Jr.

1908   Born in New York City, May 21

1924   Graduated from Trinity School, New York City

1928   Graduated from Amherst College

      Prepared for ordination at the General Theological Seminary

1932   Ordained deacon

1933-1934 Ordained priest, served as Fellow and Tutor at the General Seminary and earned STB and STM degrees

1934   Married Lucie Culver Gould in New York City. Their children are Stephen, Philip, Duncan, Lydia and Bruce.

1934-1939 Parish priest, Trinity Church, Saint Louis, Missouri

1939-1942 Parish priest, St. John's, Northampton, Massachusetts

1942-1947 Chaplain and Chairman of the Department of Religion, Columbia University

1944-1945 Chaplain, United States Naval Reserve

1947   Consecrated Bishop of Olympia (western Washington State), June 11, 1947, Seattle, Washington

1947-1959 Bishop of the Diocese of Olympia

1960-1964	First Anglican Executive Officer, based in London; Bishop in charge, The Convocation of American Churches in Europe
1964-1968	First Vice-President of the Executive Council and Director of the Overseas Department of the Episcopal Church
1968-1970	First Vice-President of the Executive Council and the Presiding Bishop's Deputy for Program
1970-1973	Adjunct Professor of Mission and of Ascetical Theology at the General Theological Seminary; Assistant to the Rector of Trinity Parish
1972-1973	Dean of the General Theological Seminary
1974	Died in Puerto Rico, January 18

REFERENCES

References to the Bibliography are to *Stephen Bayne — A Bibliography,* privately printed in 1978. Inquiries about the Bibliography may be addressed to the Library of the General Theological Seminary, 175 Ninth Avenue, New York, New York, 10011.

Where not otherwise indicated the prayers are unpublished prayers of Bishop Bayne's.

PAGE	SOURCE	BIBLIOGRAPHY
7	*Response: Bible Readings and Intercessions for Mission, May-June 1972.* Cincinnati: The Forward Movement Publications, 1972, p. 3. Intercession for Monday, May 1, Saints Philip and James.	A32.
9	*Gifts of the Spirit.* New York: The Women's Auxiliary to the National Council, 1943, pp. 18-19.	A4.
11	*Three untitled addresses on Freedom.* Delivered during the Cranbrook Conference, Diocese of Michigan, Cranbrook, Michigan, June, 1959.	D46.
	Response: Bible Readings and Intercessions for Mission, May-June 1972, op. cit., p. 19. Intercession for Monday, May 15.	A32.
13-14	*Sorting Out What We Want. The Making of a Person Series (3).* Preached on Lift Up Your Hearts, British Broadcasting Corporation, London, England, 14 March 1962.	E182.
	Response: Bible Readings and Intercessions for Mission, May-June 1972, op. cit., p. 10. Intercession for Sunday, May 7.	A32.
15	*Our Response to God: Far and Near, May-June 1966.* Cincinnati: The Forward Movement Publications, 1966, p. 42. Meditation for Saturday, May 21.	A28.
	A Dial of Parables. Sixteen prayers for an hourly cycle, not completed and previously unpublished. The prayer for 8 o'clock (0800) in the morning.	

17   *Saint Paul's Chapel Bulletin.* Columbia   G3.
      University, New York, New York,
      28 April 1946.

      Response: Bible Readings and Intercessions   A32.
      for Mission, May-June 1972, op. cit., p.
      58. Intercession for Saturday, June 17.

19   *Response: Bible Readings and Intercessions*   A32.
      for Mission, May-June 1972, op. cit., p.
      14. Meditation and Intercession for
      Thursday, May 11, The Ascension.

20-21 *Mindful of the Love: The Holy Commu-*   A20.
      nion and Daily Life by Stephen F.
      Bayne, copyright ©1962 Oxford
      University Press Inc. Reprinted by
      permission.

23   *The Dying of the Lord Jesus.* A sermon   E158.
      on the occasion of the celebration of
      the tenth anniversary of the con-
      secration of Lauriston L. Scaife as
      Bishop of the Diocese of Western
      New York, preached in the Polish
      National Catholic Cathedral,
      Buffalo, New York, 11 May 1958.

24-25 *Saint Paul's Chapel Bulletin, op. cit.,* 3   G3.
      November 1946.

27   *PIE,* Bishop Bayne's letter to the   G5.
      clergy of the Diocese of Olympia, III
      Advent, 11 December 1955.

28   *Saint Paul's Chapel Bulletin, op. cit.*   G3.

29-36 *Unto Us Is Born This Day.* Twenty-four   A33.
      prayers for an hourly cycle beginning
      on Christmas Eve. Chelsea Square,
      New York: Privately printed,
      Christmas 1972.

27   *Convocation Newsletter, Epiphany 1964,*
      written for the congregations of the
      Convocation of American Churches
      in Europe.

38	From a sermon on the Transfiguration, preached in Trinity Church, New York City, 8 August 1971.	E249.
	Response: Bible Readings and Intercessions for Mission, May-June 1972, op. cit., p. 54. Intercession for Tuesday, June 13.	A32.
39	*Saint Paul's Chapel Bulletin, op. cit.* 26 January 1947	G3.
	A Dial of Parables, op. cit. The prayer for the Third Hour, 9 o'clock (0900) in the morning.	
41	*The Olympia Churchman.* Diocese of Olympia, Seattle, Washington. October 1947.	G4.
42-43	*Saint Paul's Chapel Bulletin, op. cit.,* 12 January 1947.	G3.
44-50	*Our Daily Course.* Twenty-four prayers for an hourly cycle beginning at midnight. New York: Privately printed, 1 January 1968.	A31.
51-52	*Saint Paul's Chapel Bulletin, op. cit.,* 2 February 1947.	G3.
	Response: Bible Readings and Intercessions for Mission, May-June 1972, op. cit., p. 46. Intercession for Tuesday, June 6.	A32.
53	*Mission Is Response.* MRI Resource Book 2. New York: The Seabury Press, 1966, p. 14.	A27.
	PIE, weekly newsletter. Office of the Bishop, Diocese of Olympia, Seattle, Washington. 17 April 1955, on the occasion of the discovery of the Salk vaccine for polio.	G5.
55	*Three untitled addresses on Freedom, op. cit.*	D46.
	Response: Bible Readings and Intercessions for Mission, May-June 1972, op. cit., p. 18. Intercession for Sunday, May 14.	A32.

56-57	From an untitled sermon on the occasion of the Service of Thanksgiving for the Ministry of Erville B. Maynard. Preached at Christ Church, Grosse Pointe, Michigan, 20 April 1969.	E235.
58-65	*The Day of the Passion.* Twenty-four prayers for an hourly cycle beginning at 6 p.m. on Maundy Thursday. New York, New York, Lent 1968.	I6.
67	*The Optional God.* New York: 1953 Oxford University Press, Inc. 1980 Morehouse-Barlow Co., Inc., Paperback edition, p. 86.	A7.
68	Ibid., p. 6	A7.
69-73	*A Dial of Parables, op. cit.*	
74-75	*Mission is Response, op. cit.,* pp. 68-69	A27.
77	*Convocation Newsletter, op. cit.* January 17, 1961.	
78	From an untitled sermon preached in Christ Church, Grosse Pointe, Michigan, 20 April 1969.	E235.
79	*The Bishop's Address.* Delivered during the Forty-Ninth Annual Meeting of the Convention of the Diocese of Olympia, Seattle, Washington, 20-23 May 1959.	D45.
80	From an address at an Overseas Mission Society meeting in Philadelphia, date unknown.	
81	From *The Tree and The Man,* circulated to the clergy of the Diocese of Olympia, Seattle, Washington, Christmas 1959.	E175.

ACKNOWLEDGMENTS

Book design: Thomas Goddard
Appreciation is also expressed to Peggy Chisholm, editor of
Stephen Bayne — A Bibliography, *for her helpful*
advice and generous assistance.